Life Transforming Generosity

By Wadid Daoud

LIFE TRANSFORMING GENEROSITY

Cover: A child in Guatemala who benefited from one of the author's programs.

ISBN 979-8-218-51350-4

Manufactured in the United States of America
First printing September 2024

Contents

Generosity?

What do you think of when the word *generosity* is tossed around?

The word seems to have a different connotation to everyone, but the simple definition is the virtue to be liberal and lavish in your giving. Giving without abandon is extremely freeing and liberating.

So why is generosity so important? Because there are immeasurable aspects to giving and life altering lessons to be expected and experienced when you live your generous life now.

I will take you through my journey of generosity over the past five decades and share how it formed my world viewpoint and my inner being. This is a lifelong marathon not a 100-yard sprint, taking a lot of courage, discipline and endurance. It will reveal who you truly are and challenge every pre-set idea on which you have shaped your life. This is not about just giving financially; it is about investing your time, talent and treasure to bring about significant life-changing events. Your generosity is not about your money but all about the people whose lives – including yours – will be radically transformed.

Your generous giving is not about how much

you do and give but how much it costs you to do it. This is ultimately not about defining generosity, but rather how generosity ends up defining you.

The Beginning

My earliest recollection of generosity begins when I was about 7 or 8 years old in Cairo, Egypt. My beloved mother would take my brother and I to distribute sweets once a week to the poor children after their church-free meal. I remember feeling special as I was distributing the candy, probably experiencing joy from the smiles and happiness demonstrated in return from these children.

I was brought up in middle class family and had many challenges as did everyone else since our nation was at war and there were shortages of everything. Our parents and neighbors had to stand in long lines to get basic foodstuffs, tea and sugar. I also remember my grandfather Abouna Marcos Daoud, who lived three floors above us in our Heliopolis apartment; he would host a barrage of guests who would come over for prayers and would also ask to borrow money so they could get by. He never turned away anyone and was always happy to help, giving away all his savings. He always said if you loan money, do it without expecting it to come back. Most of it never came back, and he was ok with that and never held it against anyone who asked even if they received money multiple times. He also never brought it up or kept track of who he "lent" to. As long as he could, he was always generous with his time and treasures. Everyone felt welcomed, and they loved my grandfather and reveled in his company. Some neighbors visited him daily to just say hello or have a cup of tea and spend time with him. He was very wise and everyone that came always asked him for advice which again he gave freely.

A few years later, we left Egypt because of religious persecution and started our globetrotting journey in Accra, Ghana. I guess I was too young to understand it all and just rolled with the idea of starting a new life in a strange country where we knew no one and I did not speak the language. There the food situation was worse to the point that we had to drive to the neighboring country Togo to buy basic foods. My mother learned to improvise and cook a lot of the vegetables and fruits that we grew in the backyard. We always got by and fed our household staff.

On weekends, we would drive to the beach. On the way to the final stretch, we would encounter a young boy just waiting on the side of the road outside his village for someone to stop and pick them up. Dad always stopped, and we brought him with us to spend the day and treated him like he was part of the family. We would share our food with him, and he would climb the coconut trees and get some down for the whole family to enjoy.

In West Africa, Ghana once was one of the main slavery shipping ports along with Liberia, so there was a subdued racial tension, and the foreign community kept to itself and their distance from the locals. Not in our house, though. We hosted and friended the locals and treated our staff fairly and shared whatever we had with them. As mom experimented with cooking, she made a pound cake one day as a treat and thought she was teaching our cook Jack. When it was baked and we all tried it, she realized she had forgotten to add the sugar and told Jack, his reply was "Yes sir, madam I know." He agreed but would have never volunteered this information when she was preparing it. We ate it all anyway, as nothing was ever wasted or thrown away. We also had a huge mango tree in the backyard, and when it produced the harvest there were hundreds of mangoes that my brother and I collected. Mom figured out many ways to take advantage of that bounty by making ice cream, jam and chutneys that we feasted on for months.

I also remember a trip to Nairobi, Kenya, on our

way to Ethiopia to visit my aunt. After a long plane journey, we reached our hotel, and mom decided to take my brother and I for dinner to a nearby Indian restaurant. Shortly after we ordered and an order of four samosas had come out, a beggar came over and asked for money. Without hesitation, mom offered him a samosa, which he kindly accepted. Then he handed it back over and asked her if she could put some salt on it, which she did and returned it to him. As he starts eating it, a distinguished gentleman who had seen all this transpire shoos him away and apologizes for what just happened. The entertainment was just about to begin. He somehow invited himself to sit with us and began by telling us he can foresee the future. It began with the weather; he said he would hit the post he was sitting next to three times, and it would start raining. As soon as he did that, it started pouring down. Then went on to read my brother's palm. He would claim my brother, who at the time was probably nine or so, would be an architect and a builder. My brother studied business administration and went to work for an aftermarket automotive transmission company in international sales. So, it looked for years that this gentleman was way off. It took 25 years for his prediction to come through, as out of nowhere my brother developed a love for construction and architecture, which started by building his horse ranch, then my parent's home, followed by various industrial warehouses, single family homes, and even an apartment building. Because my mother offered a beggar a samosa, what followed was peculiar and not expected.

My mother's kindness and larger than life persona was forming us. Generosity is taught and passed down from generation to generation. We live in a tough world where there is very little space for generosity, as we evolve from survival of the fittest to reaching out to be as wealthy and comfortable as we can, even at the expense of others. That world does not have any consideration for compassion, empathy or justice. Generosity cuts through all our prejudices and brings our humanity to the forefront.

The Process and Foundation

As the years passed, I found myself following my grandfather's and parents' footsteps. I decided to do a deep dive and find out every aspect of this generosity. It has been said, it is more blessed to give than to receive. That statement is so counter-intuitive, so I decided to put it to the test. That is especially true for the poor, for what can they give? I will try to unpack this for us. Most people give because it makes them feel good about their action or to be acknowledged by their community. Most also give out of their abundance and do it impulsively. The generosity journey starts with discovery not giving. You might think the discovery is about the cause you will give to, but that is not the first step. It starts with getting to know the giver, yourself, a deep dive into who you truly are because generosity is not something you do, it is an expression of who you are. Spend as much time as you need to find out what makes you who you are. Everyone on this planet is unique, therefore there is not another person alive that can find out or draw you a guide to your discovery journey.

Where to begin? We are shaped by our past experiences and our intellect. Our intellect is our processing center that allows us to analyze right from wrong and the way we develop our peace that allows us to live with ourselves. It lets us know how far we can push or be pushed. It defines our non-negotiables and prejudices. What we experience and how we process things will establish our worldview. Most of the time, it is a half full or half empty glass of water worldview. Is that the correct way to go about this? I would challenge you to dig deep and reach a harmonious peaceful and steady viewpoint that does not pendulum according to your feelings or circumstances. Part of that knowing yourself and defining your world viewpoint is the commitment to be true to yourself. What do I mean by that? You must always come back to who you are, even if it is not popular or has dire consequences at work or to your relationships. Being true to yourself is a conviction by which you live, your life compass.

This discovery of you is the most important step in this process. If you find out that you do not like the you, you are you can put steps in place to change your weaknesses and build on your strengths. Remember, you are unique, and only you can discover you and do this. You can shape who you want to be regardless of who you are today and fill that list with good virtues such as truth, honesty, kindness and generosity. Once that is established and you commit to be true, these virtues hence be true to who you are. All of these are honorable virtues, so why should generosity make the list? It is not because of how it makes you feel. It made the list because it will enrich your life beyond anything you have ever experienced.

When I was 30 years old, I decided to continue down the journey and test its fundamental truths. I had started my own business a couple of years earlier and leaving the security of corporate America to venture into entrepreneurship. Although most businesses do not make it through the first five years, I was blessed and actually earned more in my first year than my best year in corporate America. So, I thought hard about how to be generous with my time, talent and treasures. The first thing was to deploy my non-negotiable virtues of justice and fairness. I felt this injustice growing up by seeing other suffer to no fault of their own and personally experienced it when coming to the United States and in corporate America. My quest was to focus on the unfortunate ones who did nothing to deserve the circumstance which they found themselves in, widows and orphans. Most widows depended on the providing of their late husband; one day he was gone, and they found themselves hopeless and helpless with multiple children to care for and not enough to go around. Orphans are even more vulnerable as the parents that brought them to this world are not present, they have no one to care for them and become a burden to society and are treated worse than any household pet. In some countries, they are hunted and killed like wild animals as they forage through the garbage dumps. What did they do to deserve such a life except be born to unfavorable circumstances?

These are the least of our society, and treated like a burden or worse a disease that needs to be eradicated. That infuriates my inner being. As I write this, a flood of emotions flow through my inner being from anger to compassion driven by empathy. The cruelty of our humanity plays out in that arena daily, hourly and minute by minute. So having found myself and defining my values and virtues, it was time to put a plan together to shed a little hope and a ray of sunshine on this grave matter. That project frankly took center stage to my growing business. The geographical area that I had visited for the last decade and now was making my living from was the prime offender of such injustice and lack of care for its orphans and widows. Central America rivaled some parts of

Africa in poverty and social injustice. The first step was to research and find out all I could about the complexity of this phenomenon and who the players are in that arena.

Once the research was completed, it was time to deploy my talents. I knew I did not just want to write a check to a reputable charity and feel good about doing something. So, I visited five local charities working in that region and started my due diligence on all of them. My business acumen, one of my gifts, helped in determining the impact each charity was having on my orphans and widows in that region. Notice I claimed them as if they were my responsibility, I owned this process and had to see it through. I am not delusional and understand perfectly well that I cannot eradicate this, but all I started out to do was share a ray a hope and a drop of love with them. After a round of interviews, I narrowed the search to a couple of charities; after all, why reinvent the wheel and start my own if someone else could do the work to my satisfaction? There are charities all around the world that reach out to every aspect of life including fauna and flora. Be aware that not all are good, hence the due diligence.

After a second interview, I determined the charity that I was going to deploy was Food for the

Poor, but was not sold on any of the work they did as it did not line up with what I wanted to accomplish. So, I tasked them with coming up with a project that would initially feed the widows and orphans and had to be self-sustaining (meaning I would only invest once and not have to keep pouring money into it to succeed). On my next visit, they presented me with a half a dozen projects, but most of them were labor intensive, and some had too many variables to ensure their success. I wanted to eliminate all the variables as the recipients should not have to deal with any hardship. Finally, the charity reluctantly showed me a project designed by a Jesuit priest in Guatemala that was not proven (they had never done it before) but was the perfect fit for what I envisioned – soy milk processing mini plants.

We put together a list of items including a solar panel, a pot, burners, piping and bags to process soy. That would be nutritious and healthy and sustainable. Guatemala is a producer of soy, so it was available locally. They put together a local team through Caritas Catholic charities to identify the needy to receive the projects, install and train the recipients to use them, and provided them with recipes to make milk, cheese, pancakes, sausage, ice cream etc. Once we agreed on the project, the charities fees and feasibility, they presented me with final draft of the scope of work and a budget of $35,000 that they would need in full to start.

I was pleased with their proposal, however, there was one glitch – I did not have $35,000 in my bank account to fund the project but nevertheless committed to getting it on the spot. I do not know where that conviction came from but felt that a way would present itself to fund this. A week later, I receive a call from one of our vendors asking me to quote a client who had reached out to them directly. I did not know the client or ever heard of them before, they asked for a product that was not available to U.S. distributors and was only available in Europe. I called the vendor, and he said they would sell it me and gave me guidance on where to price it. I quoted the client around $65,000 for cash deal, since I did not know them. They accepted and sent the funds, so I called my factory salesman and advised him I had the order and asked him what it would cost me. I had not inquired before as these quotes normally do not amount to anything except a waste of time. He did not ask me what I sold it for but came back to me and said, "I looked at our cost, and we can sell you the deal for $28,000, will that work?" "Absolutely," I replied and thanked him. He did not know that is what I needed to fund our first of many soy projects.

The next step was getting on a plane and traveling with an agent of the Food for the Poor to Guatemala to meet the local partner Caritas that would implement the project and introduce us to the recipients of the projects, so I could confirm the need and impact. After the projects were operational, a second trip to evaluate their success and identify more recipients.

The reason I share this story with you is because that was the beginning of my journey where generosity showed up and toughed me it was not about me or what I had. If my heart was right, everything would fall into place and I get to witness Greatness in spite of me and my resources. We went on to build more than 30 soy processing plants with a huge impact on the poor of that region.

Find a cause that you are passionate about and pursue it with the same zeal as you would your business or family or whatever you hold dear to you.

The Why

I have thought long and hard about the why, and the short answer is because it benefits us more than the recipient. How that works out is really a mystery. Most religions instruct you to give so you can be blessed, mainly financially. But that should not be the reason to be generous. Generosity starts as a learned habit and eventually becomes part of who you are. Being generous is not something you do as the opportunity presents itself. It is a lifestyle by which you are always in tune with the opportunities as they frequent your daily life. Let us say you want to be part of the elite squad at the Olympic Games. That is also a very long journey. It starts with a commitment to train every day, eat right and get into a regiment that will get you ready to compete. Then there is the local competition followed by the state then the region. Once you get through these, then the national team is followed by the international. You must really love what you are doing and be focused to get all the way to the Olympics. Once you get there at the opening ceremony, the feeling is unreal, as you are participating as an elite member of the most prestigious sporting event on the planet. The emotions of joy and happiness that culminated from all these years of training are finally coming to reality. On the day of your event, the excitement is unbearable, and the whole world is watching you as you do what you have prepared for years if not decades. Just participating is a tremendous honor, but winning a medal, especially a gold, is elating. Generosity is a similar journey, with a lot of hard work and ups and downs, but the final result if your heart is right is always a gold medal and an overwhelming joy and peace that comes upon you for doing the work and finishing the race. Many climbers, when asked "Why do you climb mountains that are dangerous?" answer because it is there. Many generous people will answer this question in various ways. There are many reasons that drive generous people to giving and doing the work. Some of the most common are:

1. I reacted to a need and gave.
2. There's no one doing the work and a need to set up a charity or a cause to solve this issue.
3. The need is overwhelming, and the workers are few, so I'll roll up my sleeves and jump in.
4. I have the heart and an overwhelming burden to do something to alleviate the issue.

17

5. I have been blessed, and now it is time to give back.
6. My friend or community is doing a project and I will join them. Social belonging.

All of these are good and a valid answer why to be generous could be the beginning of the training, but ultimately it is because you are training to win the Gold Medal at the Olympics of Generosity, a lifelong marathon of experiences that will mold and shape who you are...where you can look back and see that you are much better than when you started...a better person because of the work generosity did in your life just like the training did in the athlete's life to make them stronger and faster. You will gain a different perspective on life and with that comes vision, drive, wisdom, discernment, intuition, endurance, peace and joy.

The Vision

Visionaries are persons with original ideas about what the future would look like. They can see and even experience that future in their mind. Once that vision is set, it starts to gnaw at them pushing them to put a plan together for action. When I was in my late thirties, I had a vision of striking poverty at a school that was run by a Korean order of nuns in Guatemala. I had met these nuns through the soy milk project and visited many times since that had taken place. Over dinner at one of my visits, I went on a deep dive as to why and how they got started in Guatemala. The story was fascinating, and their heart of generosity was impeccable. They sacrificed everything to bring hope to these young boys and girls who would never have an education and maybe even die from malnutrition. As I write this, my heart still breaks, as the need is great and the resources are few. I learned that their calling was to go to the most remote areas of the country and find the poorest families and offer their children a free but most excellent education at their first-class facility in Guatemala City. Boys' Town houses 4,000 boys and Villa de las Ninas houses around 3,000 girls. I asked the sisters what happens to the children once they graduate? Their answer was very unsettling, as they shared that most of them go back to their villages to help their parent in the field, or get odd jobs to get by. After that conversation, my mind started on a what if journey. I started forming a vision to give these 18-year-old a better future. The vision was to strike at their generational poverty and give them a brighter future where they could break the bondage that they were destined to.

Over the next few weeks, as I thought about it and considered various options that included adding more resources to the sisters of Maria for a college-type education. I came up with a scholarship program that the sisters would implement and offer to 12 graduating students of their choosing. So, I shared it with them and they were excited to put it to practice starting the end of that school year, they also agreed to administer the program and distribute the funds accordingly. They came up with a budget for 12 students to continue their education and go to a university and study whatever they wanted with the guidance of the sisters. The cost at the time was approximately $1,500 a student yearly with a four-year commitment as long as they maintained their grades. The plan was to fund the first 12 students' year one and add 12 more each year after that. So, in year one, we would fund 12, year two 24, year three 36, and year four 48 students then from year five on, it would remain at 48 students as the first graduates were replaced by the new students. As I studied the numbers and received a profile of each student with their chosen career, I was excited to get started. I knew I would need help raising the funds, so I thought it would be great to send a proposal to my business distributors with the plan as well as a profile of each student, similar to sponsoring a child charity World Vision. I did not come up with that but choose to use someone else's concept that would work for this project. Do not reinvent the wheel; if there is something out there that works use it.

I sent the e-mail to more than 50 distributors. To my utter disappointment, only two replied and committed to a four-year sponsorship of one student. I know that was a great setback, but I had promised the nuns that we would fund 12 students and could not let them down. Sometimes in life when you are in a situation like that, tough choices have to be made. The easy way out would have been to scrap the program until we had the funds, maybe push it out one more year, but the problem with that is I gave my word and everything was in place and the students were excited and the sisters engaged. I decided to push forward and fund the 10 students myself. Remember what I said at the beginning – your generosity will define you.

This was the second defining moment of supernatural provision. What I mean about that is the money was going to be provided just like it was last time with soy projects, and I had no idea from where or how but I was ready to be astonished. I really cannot put my finger on a specific event that funded this project, but I can remember that we never lacked the funds month in month out. I would like to tell you that this project is still ongoing, however due to many changes at the schools and other circumstances, it only went on for about six years. That you could say in our economy is a failure, however, in a later visit to Boys Town, the sister had gathered 12 of the students that had graduated over dinner and had them share the transformation of their lives. My wife and I were in tears over what we heard; some were tears of joy and most for the struggle and injustice of this broken world we live in. That was a confirmation that what we did was worthwhile and had accomplished the mark.

The most impactful story that will stay with me

forever was a young man who was 8 years old when the nuns found him polishing shoes in his village to scrounge enough money to contribute to his family's survival. They took him in. He had graduated as a lawyer and had secured a good job at a local law firm and was sending money back to his family to help them out. He never in his wildest dreams imagined that his life would turn out that way. The sisters through their visionary generosity, started his journey (as well as those of thousands of others), and we were able to alter his destined outcome from a survival, poverty and possible starvation to a successful, wholesome thriving life. That is seeing your vision come to completion.

The Drive

At some point in everyone's life, the big questions start to brew in our mind, as we wonder why we are here on this planet and ultimately what our life here is all about. Are we just passing through, and what are we supposed to accomplish? This is the beginning of a very fundamental formation that will define what we will accomplish while here. We will strive, survive, or just give up. Giving up is the easy way out; it is like signing up for a marathon without knowing why you did it and never training for it. The day of the marathon comes, and you may show up or skip it all together as it was just a passing thought and did not plan on really participating much the less finishing the race. Unfortunately, many people fall in this category and just give up on life, some by taking drastic measures of ending it early. There are many steps that drive to these results; not all of them self-inflicted, as some come from outside pressures that the individual is not capable to deal with and sees no way out. Others just show up for the race, run a little, walk a little more, then when the whole field has passed them by, give up and go home filled with disappointment and regret.

Giving up on life is deeply rooted in our inner being, especially as we face disappointment or loss. Overcoming that, although difficult, is a reachable goal, as we move to the next step of just surviving. We do show up at the start line and are able to grind through the race; it is tough, and at moments we want to give up. Instead, we walk some but then slowly continue pushing through but not really enjoying it. It feels like a burden more than a joyous experience. It is all about surviving and getting to the end, mile by mile, while missing all the beauty around us and not interacting with the other runners along the way. A very lonely journey of hard grind that seems meaningless. Most of the population of Third World countries find themselves in this situation, as their only goal is to find enough food to get through another day. Finally, we get to an elite group of athletes that have prepared daily, sacrificed loads to get into the race, not just to finish but to do it well. That takes drive to get up early every morning to stretch and train, to keep your mind focused, to eat healthy, to take out of your life any and everything that gets in the way of your goal. The race is equally grueling on mind and body. The mind has to be in the right frame to thrive and drive the body. It is very important not to ignore your mental ability to thrive while getting your body ready for the race. Also, a balance of work and rest is key to success. Most people we admire in life that have accomplished great things have that drive; they do not give up.

Still, some of them have tragic ends, as their drive leads them to an insignificant end and meaningless results. That is why it's very important that your drive to thrive must be anchored in a truth that cannot be shaken or diluted to meaningless. The key to thriving in your drive is to keep your eye on a prize that is life-altering and fulfilling. How does that drive relate to generosity? Giving of yourself as you embark on your journey is the anchor that gives meaning to your race.

Let me explain how that looks like in real life. If your anchor is about making and accumulating as much money as you can in this life, a very lonely and sad outcome will follow. Every friendship will be put to the test, as you will never be sure if they like you because of your wealth and how it benefits them. You will be very busy and guarded trying to protect your wealth. In the end, you become a slave to the anchor you have set. That is why your anchor needs to bring you freedom not enslave you. There is nothing more freeing than to give away your time, talent and treasure.

I have wrestled with that notion over time and truly believe that through every event (good and bad) that life has brought my way was meant to be unpacked, analyzed and used as a valuable life lesson. For example, I was approached years ago about investing in a company that had a proprietary molecule that would treat any skin disorder. Looking over the business plan, all I could think about was the outsized returns on investment and started putting in motion a very aggressive plan to provide a sustainable water project to every tribe in Africa that did not have that basic need available. Well, I had invested a sacrificial amount praying over the investment to reach the goal of being able to invest it all at the end in the water project. To my surprise and utter shock, a year later, I ended up losing everything and getting sued for even more money. That was a very painful but necessary lesson that took me years to unpack and learn from. My biggest hang-up was not the heartburn of how things turned out but the why. I could not reconcile that my good intentions to alleviate suffering of others had been squandered without any results. At the end, you can say that was lack of wisdom on my part, or an even great gamble that did not pay off. But the how I dealt with it is what the drive is all about. At this critical juncture, I could have given up, been bitter and never venture down that road again. However, years later all that money that was invested was made whole through other paths. I cannot account for it all but know that it was a learning lesson that I needed to heed to be able to thrive. Every one of us is under a time clock in this world, and whatever we accumulate in this life will not follow us in to the next, so why not invest it wisely to right some wrongs that will benefit others. Are most of us so self-centered and selfish that we miss the greater good? That comes down to the fundamental questions that we all end up answering about why we are here. It really comes down to roads to benefit and indulge ourselves or to leave this place better than we found it. If we take the later road greater riches await us and we will have run a good race and finished well.

Wisdom

There are many books, including Proverbs, that have a lot to say about wisdom. I am going to define it as it pertains to generosity. It is being able to discern and have a good sense of judgment as it relates to your giving. Remember the investment I made to get to develop the water project that never happened? Did you ever find an investment that you thought was bulletproof and returns were so outrageous that you got blinded by the returns and did not seek wise counsel? That was lack of wisdom on my part. Maybe if I would have shared this with a mentor or a financial advisor other than the one offering the deal, things would have turned out differently. While I consider putting that in the lack of wisdom bucket, the lesson learned helped me seek wisdom before I would venture down another risky start-up to fund a project. I have learned not to risk hard earned money in unproven investments that would be earmarked for giving. There is no get rich quick scheme that works even though your intentions are honorable and selfless. Wisdom is a gift that is given if you seek it. It does not come naturally to everyone and eludes most people through their journey on earth.

Seek a mentor, as that will aid you on your way to seeking wisdom, two heads are better than one. The mentor must be someone that you value and respect and that will be truthful and honest with you without being judgmental or envious. If you can put a group of solid mentors in your life it will truly enrich your decision making. You will need all the wisdom you can muster to make sure your generosity is on the right track and effective. Many people mistake generosity for tipping. Generosity requires a sacrifice on your part. Tipping is a token of your plenty. Some of the wisdom I have acquired through this journey:

1. Success without a generous life in a futile journey.
2. One must dig deep to be able to develop a generous heart.
3. The way of generosity will set you free.
4. Develop a group of mentors to guide your decisions.
5. Share your journey's highs and lows with your family and friends.
6. Always assess where you are on the path.

Discernment

How do you apply discernment to generosity? Think of it as a new business venture or a great investment idea that you were presented or came up with. Would you just sign the contract and hand over your hard-earned cash without vetting it? Or you would spend countless hours learning about the industry, visiting the different players in that arena, seeing and studying their successes and their failures, meeting with the management team to see if they are competent or up to the task. In your discernment journey of generosity, you must exercise the same manner of rigorous vetting, remember you are not about to invest in a life or world changing venture without securing its success. Discernment is beyond doing all of the above, it is the ability to know whether to go forward or change direction. That comes with spending a lot of time meditating and reflecting on what you are about to embark on. When I was considering all the different projects that were on offer, how did I know which one to choose? I did not make my decision hastily but took time to reflect on each one until I found peace with my choice. It was an unproven project, so the success rate was greatly diminished. Nevertheless, once I spent time mediating and seeking clarity, it was clear to me that was the one I must pursue. There are many good ideas and projects out there, but discerning which is the best one for you to implement is the real challenge. How do gain discernment? Life experiences weigh in but there is more to it as one must seek solitude and weigh all options. Sometimes in life, you have to make these decisions on the fly.

I remember taking a taxi from the airport to work to pick up my car and go fetch my family. Upon arriving, the driver tried to print the receipt to accept the credit card payment, but he could not make it work, and I was in a hurry. My first thought was if he cannot make it work that is his problem and I do not need to waste my time to get him paid. I also know that these drivers wait for hours to pick up at the airport and might get two rides a day. At that point, I had to make a decision to either walk away and leave him or exercise much needed patience and wait until he could figure out how to reset his meter. I decided to show him grace and wait for over 30 minutes while he tried over and over again to reset his meter. The ride from the airport was less than the time I waited to get him paid. Up to that point, I was just exercising being a stand-up good guy. What followed was the discernment of generosity. My next struggle was do I just pay the fare and leave? After all, I wasted half an hour with my family waiting because of his inefficiency. This is where my generosity kicked in, and I literally put myself in his place. He deserved my wrath and leaving without paying the fare, and he would not expect a tip after all that happened. Instead, I decided to tip him on top of the regular fare, which surprised him, and he was grateful.

Have you ever been inconvenienced and decided to take it out on the clerk attending you when your plane is delayed or your food is late and cold? Generosity is not about the tip; it is about behaving in a way that shows others that they are valued when the circumstances are obviously not in their favor. Encouraging the gate attendant with a kind word and let them know they are valued even though they are the bearer of bad news that the flight is delayed or even canceled and everyone else is cursing them and screaming at them. Discernment will give you a different perspective on the situations you find yourself in and will feel counterintuitive at first but will grow and alter your views and actions if you let it. The reality is you can only control yourself; there are situations that are beyond your control, and these you do not need to worry about because you will not alter their course. Take a hurricane, for example, that is barreling your direction. Worrying about it will not alter the hurricane's course or get you ready to face it. The only thing you can control is your decision – either stay put to ride it out or flee. The same applies to a canceled flight; screaming at the gate attendant is not going to reinstate the flight. You can get up calmly and go rebook on another flight instead of abusing others out of your frustration and getting furious over something that is out of your control. That is why discernment and generosity go hand in hand. Once you have discerned the right path, a small act of generosity can diffuse an explosive situation and now you are standing up for the gate attendant, the waiter, and the taxi driver.

Intuition

Intuition is the ability to know or understand something immediately without conscious reasoning. How intuition interacts with generosity is quite unique and very rewarding. I remember an instance in the late 1980s, while on a business trip to Honduras, when I decided to venture into San Pedro Sula city center for dinner on my own instead of just dining at the hotel in the outskirt of town. I found a pizza place and sat by the sidewalk. As I sat down, a boy about eight years old walked up to me and asked if he could shine my shoes. I agreed as I usually got my shoes shined in my travels. We started talking about him and his family when all of a sudden, I decided to invite him to dine with me. He asked if his brother could join us, and I accepted. So, he went to fetch him as I instructed the waiter to set up two more settings on the table, as I was expecting company. The three of us shared a meal, some laughter and stories. The restaurant owner did not look too pleased but allowed it and said nothing. It was not what I expected when I left the hotel that evening, however, it was it most enjoyable dinner I had on that trip not because the food was the best but because the company was. You can call that judgment or lack of it risky, and the result could have turned out very differently, but my intuition was to share a memorable hour or so with unfortunate children that fit right perfectly with my passion. It was not planned or rehearsed; it just happened. To me, it is still one the memories I have left and cherish, as I do not remember most of my past as my memory has been fragmented since my two head-on automobile collisions.

How did I know to invite these two boys and share a meal with them? That is intuition making an immediate decision without consciously thinking it through. Not all intuitive acts of generosity are rewarded equally; some are just totally ignored, and that is fine. I was not doing this for a feel-good moment, and if these boys would have left unappreciative and bitter, I would have still done the same, as in my mind it was the right thing to do and aligned with my heart to alleviate the least of our society's subsistent existence. I do not know how this evening played in their future development and probably will never find out, but at least for me and being true to myself, I planted a seed in their lives that hopefully gave them hope in mankind even if it was just for a moment in their lifetime. There are many opportunities to be generous in our daily journey; some require planning and being very deliberate, and others just require an intuitive touch. Both are equally impactful; however, the intuitive acts do help build up the endurance for the long journey of enduring projects that you develop.

Endurance

Endurance can best be described as to when you have reached the point where you can no longer go on, you keep pushing through. Endurance is the ability to see us through life's struggles, infirmities, trials, hardship or adversity. You see endurance is not a plan to stand strong most of the time it is a moment by moment resolve not to give up. Most of us have endured events that at the time seemed forever however years or decades later they are but a faint memory. Some events are more memorable and impactful than others never the less we still had to endure them. Endurance truly shows us what we are capable of. If we do not endure life's challenges and keep pushing through, we miss what our life here is all about. It is character building; it shapes you into who you are becoming and finally give you hope that this too will pass. How does this apply to generosity? I had a burning desire to alleviate the pain that widows and orphans are going through and that is not a simple one and done journey, it is one filled with heartache and longevity. There are so many opportunities to make a difference, so much need it seems overwhelming most of the time as I think about the best way to make a significant difference while my heart breaks for the suffering. The easy way out would be to just write a check and move on and think about something else, but that is not the endurance required of this lifetime journey. I say lifetime because it only ends when we are no longer walking this Earth that is why endurance is so important. In my journey, we started by feeding the poor, then moved to educating them followed by housing them and giving them hope that they are not forgotten but loved by their fellow humans. That was all well and good and compartmentalized away from our home.

A few years ago, a totally unexpected opportunity arose that was very different. My wife and I had volunteered to go help clean and repair a foster home nearby on a Saturday. We gathered our kids and grandkids and went to help invest kindness in our community. It seemed like a good thing to do on its own. However, what followed was a twist in our lives that we had not planned for or could have foretold. At the foster home, as we were having lunch break, my wife who had spent most of the morning with two of the foster girls started talking to the foster parents. The foster mom advised her that the girls' parental rights were terminated and that they would be put up for adoption. Without missing a beat, my wife looked at me and said, "How about it babe?" I want to stress at that point that choosing a partner who shares your heart for whatever you are passionate about is very important. I was instantly onboard however we decided to consider it separately, and as I was about to leave for Panama for five days we would reconvene upon my return.

Later that Saturday, we found out that they were sisters and that there was three of them not two, as the third one was not home because she had gone to play soccer with the foster parent's daughter. The following day, I left for Panama, and we had decided not to share our thoughts about the matter until my return. This was quite a unique experience for me as I physically sat in business meetings but mentally all I could think of were the three little girls that needed a home. I thought and struggled about what to do. That was a clash between our conviction and our comfort. I kept thinking of all the reasons why we should not do it then flip-flop to all the reasons why we need to. Finally, I get home and shared my resolve with my wife with excitement. However, she was not on-board yet and needed a couple of more days to make peace with her decision. That was not a decision to make lightly no matter how excited we were and knowing our hearts were in the right place as it would be a lifelong commitment.

The following Wednesday, we called the foster charity that housed them and told them we wanted to adopt all three girls. We knew the head of the charity there who thought we were crazy and did try to dissuade us as this is not an easy journey we were about to embark on. However, we were resolute and started adoption classes that Friday. As we went through the first class, the teacher asked why we were there. I replied because we met three little girls that we are going to adopt. She laughed and went on to say there are many parents' way ahead of us in the process and these girls would be adopted before we get through the system. I looked her straight in the eye and said these girls are going to be adopted by us and left. The whole process of adoption, which usually takes years to go through took us thee months from when the girls moved in with us until they took our last name and were ours. I wish I could tell you it has been all roses and laughter, but I can say through the ups and downs endurance has brought us through. They have been part of our family now for about six years and they are thriving. Some opportunities require sacrifice and are a lifetime investment, however, through it all it has changed us to who we are today. We would not be who we are if we would have passed up this opportunity, our lives would be lacking this rich experience that shaped us.

Peace

Peace can best be described as a state of harmony, tranquility and quiet. Deep down, we all strive for peace, but it seems to elude us. I remember in 1978 when we lived in Teheran. Although I was a young boy, the revolution to remove the Shah was under way. It was utter chaos, and there were thousands of people in the street fighting the government forces and looting everything in sight. My father took us to airport to try to leave the country with the clothes on our backs. There were no banks, no gasoline, no food. Although too young to fully understand the gravity of the situation, I remember him in the madness of the airport with all foreigners trying to leave the country going from counter-to-counter pleading with the airline representatives to get us four tickets on any flight leaving the country. After the second day of tirelessly talking to all airlines, he found a sympathetic ear at the Kuwait airline counter and secured a flight to Kuwait and then a few days later to Cairo. We left the country with very little money that he had kept at home. That was two weeks before the Shah left, and 52 Americans were taken hostage. As I reflect on that period of time that shaped our family, there was a sense of urgency, anxiety and despair as the future of our family was at stake. The peace and stability that we longed for seemed unattainable. But somehow, we were able to overcome the circumstance we found ourselves in and get to safety. I know that is an extreme situation that few had to endure, but it does make you evaluate life and its fragility.

Seeking peace ought to be a priority to ensure a healthy mindset and thriving existence. Just as we crave peace in our life, we need to extend that to our generosity, as we put ourselves in the shoes of the ones we were trying to help. Their peace ought to be as important to us as our peace.

We started building houses in Guatemala for widows and their children because that extended a sense of peace and security in their arduous lives. As we have followed the progress of that project, the results were quite surprising. Most of the women we donated homes to were working tirelessly in the garbage dump collecting cardboard and plastic to recycle to survive and feed their children. Once we secured the land and built them a home, there was a change of heart and a sense of peace that took them out of their poverty and into entrepreneurship. Out of more than 50 families that received home, only three kept going back to the dump and continued as before; the rest got jobs or decided to make and sell food and products to get ahead.

There is story I would like to share about a family in a very remote area in the jungle of Central America that had two children. One day a priest goes to visit them and spends a few days with them in their humble dwelling. Over his time there, he finds out that the family had one cow and totally depended on that cow. In the morning and evening, they would milk the cow and use the milk and its derivatives to survive. Early in the morning before the family was awake, the priest packed his belonging and set out to leave. On his way, he came across the cow, killed it, and went on his way.

Years later he decided to go back and revisit the family. When he went to look for them, he could not find them. So, he wandered until he found their neighbors and inquired about the family's whereabouts. The neighbors told him that they had moved a few years back and now had a successful farm with a big house and their sons went to school and got good jobs.

As I thought of that story and discussed it with our partners in Guatemala, we had killed the cow when we started building houses around the garbage dump. In this case, the cow was the dependence on the garbage dump to survive. Now we were able to move their lives from survival to thriving, and that creates a peace in their lives.

Joy

I guess joy can best be described as that felling you get when all is well and things are going your way. However, I think joy is closely related to peace because without peace there cannot be a deep lasting joy. There might be moments of joy, but it does not last past the next change of circumstances.

How does generosity tie to joy? The act of selflessness generates joy that quenches the soul. The ability to change lives will fill your emptiness with joy. I remember feeling down and empty as a young man even though I was quite popular but that never brought me joy. It was not until I started serving others that my whole inner joy sense started to pivot. Whenever you think you have hit bottom and have nothing to give of any value, consider the multitudes of people that would trade places with you in an instant because your life is so much more bearable than theirs ever will be, yet here we are with everything and our mind has trapped us into thinking less of ourselves than what we deep down inside know we are and can do. The one thing that can liberate you is generosity; it will bring back the value to your being. If you have ever thought of giving up on your life because you are a failure or because you have obtained it all and that lead you to empty promises and dreams that evaporated and did not meet your expectation and ultimately brought you despair instead peace and joy, get up and go serve the less fortunate, show them compassion and I guarantee that will change your life and your purpose.

About 20 years ago, we were living in Wales when a unique challenge came to mind. We lived in a very rural area where sheep and cattle dominated the landscape. We were surrounded by farmers who never ventured beyond the borders of their areas. The thought behind this nugget of generosity was to bless them and let them experience a banquet like nothing that they have or would ever experience. We set out to get as many invitations out to our neighbors inviting them for a Christmas gathering. Much to our surprise, everyone replied and was excited to come. Next, we set an extravagant menu that included lobster, chateaubriand, and many dishes that were very unique from different parts of the world, all accompanied by a set of well-chosen wines, champagnes and cognac to accompany each course. We basically served four courses that included starters, main, dessert and finally a cheese. We had to order most of our provisions from London, as there was very little we could gather locally. The night of the event, the house was decorated and the tables set. Our family spent all evening serving and making sure our guests' experience was exceptional. The evening was flawless, and all had a marvelous time. I have asked myself many times if this evening was worth the investment. My conclusion was that it brought everyone involved including our family joy and that was priceless.

Ultimately, when your purpose is in the right direction and you get the vision and drive to see it through, that will be the road to peace and joy. Remember at the beginning I stated that generosity will define who you are. We are all striving toward peace and joy, and generosity is the main artery to get us there. It will move us from selfishness to selflessness and will create a pool of compassion for others to care for, dwarfing our woes and monumentally shifting our feelings of worthlessness and hopelessness to mountains of great hope and a great wealth of worth.

The Tripod That Holds It All Together

I spend time reflecting on my life and try to figure out some life truths that I lived by and that have served me well. I have come up with three crucial parts that when out of sync I cannot achieve my best life now. I call it the tripod because to stand, all three legs must equally bear weight. If one leg is broken or short, the others will not be able to hold the load on the tripod. These three key attributes that hold my life together to make me the best that I can be is the balance between my talent, time and treasure. Let me dive into this and try to show that it transcends all aspect of my life including generosity. Over the years, my life had been out of balance. When I was young, talent and treasure did not matter as it was about having a good time and my life was falling apart. When the good times ended, I had concentrated all my efforts on spending time on having a good time with my friends and nothing else to show forth. As I got older, I was on a journey to discover my talents and put them to good use. I found out that I had a unique set of talents that few had or understood, among which are the ability to see though a situation and very quickly come up with a host of possible solutions to sort through no matter how complex the situation is.

Many years ago, I was on a trip to Africa. During my travels I ended up in Sierra Leone where there, unknown to me, a civil war was erupting. When I arrived to the airport, I was forced to change $100 into local currency where the largest note was around 25 cents. I had a huge wad of notes in my brief case of local currency. There was supposed to a helicopter service from the airport to the hotel, but due to the situation it had left the country. So, I proceeded to take a taxi to the hotel. A couple of miles down the road there was a military checkpoint. The taxi driver stopped, and I was asked at gunpoint to get out of the taxi with all my belongings. At that point, I knew I was in for a unique experience. I was taken at gunpoint to a shack on the side of the road with my suitcase and briefcase. The military soldier opened the door and tried to get me in the shack where there were four more military soldiers with machine guns. One foot in the door and the other outside holding my suitcase outside, I was processing the situation. Without moving in to the shack, I started a conversation with one who looked like their leader in the room by asking who they were and what they wanted. He said they were Nigerian peace-keeping forces stuck in this war zone, then proceeded to tell me that they needed money for food. Quick on my feet, I started the negotiation for my freedom. I told him I would not move from the door and would see what I can do. I opened my brief case and took about a third of the wad of cash I had exchanged at the airport and offered it to him. He must have known that all foreigners had to change a hundred dollars upon entering the country and what that looked like in local currency. He said that was not enough, so I doubled it and tried to give him two-thirds of the cash while negotiating letting me go back to the taxi with my belongings. He refused again. So, I reached out and showed him all the money I had exchanged and he sent one of his soldiers to take it from me and told me I could leave. I quickly grabbed my bags and got in the taxi. I have thought about the different outcomes that could have taken place that day and know that one of them could have been the end of me and they would have had everything. No one would have ever found me or even known where to look. I could have been another missing person, but that day I knew my life was worth one hundred dollars. I hope I never have to find out if that price has gone up.

That same negotiating talent has served me well in my business over the years and has allowed me to prosper as well a develop some unique projects that served others. Finally, my treasure had come, as I grew older and wiser and saved in order to be able to develop my dreams. Our treasure or money I like to see it as a tool that we can use to change life. It will change lives if you direct it that way. One can spend it frivolously on themselves and their friends, but that will not bring you to the tripod that balances your life. But rather couple it with your time and talent and it could be the most powerful tool you will ever employ to make significant and everlasting change to our world and its inhabitants.

Final Thoughts

I have shared some of my journey of generosity throughout this book. It is something I am passionate about. I have thought about what I would put on my tombstone or be remembered for as my legacy. I would like it to say "He loved everyone well and gave it all for the good of others." I know my time on this earth is short. I am very aware of my treasures, and I am deploying all my talents including writing this book for a life with a greater purpose than just surviving and taking care of myself and loved ones.

I encourage you to take the challenge of sorting out your tripod by discovering your talents, managing your time wisely and putting generosity at the top of your priorities. I promise it will take you on an unforgettable journey that you will cherish for the rest of your days. It will change who you are and how you see others. It will reveal the true you with your abilities and your weaknesses. It will also prove that we are all connected more closely than we thought or imagined. It will help you develop a unique sense of intuition and wisdom. It will also give you buckets of empathy which will rock your life. Ultimately, it will give your life meaning that will lead to peace and joy.

I believe that that my generational faith and blessings started with my grandfather and seeing it in action led me to my faith and this great journey. My inner-being as well as my wellbeing rest in the hands of my beloved Jesus, who redeemed me and provided me with such a rich, meaningful and enduring life. The ultimate act of demonstrating you transformed generous life is sacrificing your life for saving the lives of others.

ABOUT THE AUTHOR

WADID DAOUD manages a variety of businesses including welding, real estate, and investments. A graduate of Letourneau University in Texas, he now resides in Fort Lauderdale, Florida. This is his first book.